Where I find God

Enjoy & Blessings

Cara,

Joanne

First published in 2016 by Columba Press
23 Merrion Square
Dublin 2
Ireland
www.columba.ie

PHOTOGRAPHY CREDITS
John Kelly: pages 10, 14, 24, 32, 38, 40, 42, 44, 48, 66, 76, 78, 94, 98, 100, 106
Norman McCloskey: pages iv, viii, xii, xiv, 4, 8, 18, 20, 26, 30, 36, 46, 52, 56, 68, 70, 74, 82, 84, 88, 92, 96, 102, 104
Christy McNamara: pages 2, 34, 54, 58, 60, 62, 90, 104
Giles Norman: pages vi, x, 6, 12, 16, 28, 50, 64, 72, 80, 86, 106, 108

POETRY CREDITS
'Place' © Fr Pádraig J. Daly. Used by kind permission of the author.
Excerpt from 'The One' by Patrick Kavanagh taken from *Patrick Kavanagh: Collected Poems* (Penguin Books, London, 2005), © The Trustees of the Estate of the late Katherine B. Kavanagh, through the Jonathan Williams Literary Agency.
Excerpt from 'In Switzerland' by Raymond Carver taken from *All of Us: The Collected Poems* (The Harvill Press, London, 1996), © Tess Gallagher.

ISBN: 978-1-78218-307-5

Set in Tisa Pro 10/13 and Atiza
Book design by Helene Pertl | Columba Press
Printed with Jellyfish Solutions

Front cover: Eagle's Nest, Killarney National Park © Norman McCloskey
Back cover: © Norman McCloskey

All royalties from the sale of this book will go to the Peter McVerry Trust and Focus Ireland.

Where I find God

CORA GUINNANE & JOANNE O'BRIEN

·····································

foreword by Mary McAleese

Contents

Image © Norman McCloskey

For Cathal, Tiarnan and Saoirse,
And Declan, Alisha, Anna, Sarah and Dylan –
In you we meet a loving God everyday.

To Peter, Marion, Liam and Annette –
Thank you for passing on the gift of faith.

Foreword

Where I Find God captures the spirituality of those living in twenty-first-century Ireland who believe in God. There is not much sign of a remote fearsome God but here is instead hope in a loving, caring God who dwells within us and all around us.

Each believer has a unique story to tell of his or her relationship with God and the variety of stories in this book underlines that uniqueness. God's extraordinary felt presence in the ordinary and the everyday, in the joys and griefs, in the easy days and the days we cannot bear to face, is also underlined throughout. As this book testifies, even the most devout believers can struggle at times to find God. Hopefully its contents will encourage and inspire, renew faith and lighten the spirit.

It is to the credit of all concerned that the proceeds from the sale of this book will go to Focus Ireland and the Peter McVerry Trust, two organisations whose founders were challenged by their faith in God to care for the homeless as you would care for a loved brother or sister – the very essence of the Christian gospel. I congratulate Cora and Joanne for bringing this project to life for such a great cause and I thank all those who have contributed in any way to its publication. Above all I hope that the men, women and children who are homeless in twenty-first-century Ireland will see in this the hands of God's work and the real possibility of a better future.

— *Mary McAleese*

Image © Norman McCloskey

ix

x

Introduction

It has been said that people come in to your life for a reason, a season or a lifetime. While we have known each other for many years, working as Secondary School Chaplains in Co. Clare, our life journeys intersected at a crossroads. Stepping away from school for a while, taking a career break allowed us the opportunity to meet more regularly. When we met we chatted about faith, God, life and the challenges Irish society is facing. We decided to take on the challenge of the Gospel and travel together to schools and parishes sharing our faith through talks, workshops and retreats. We came across many people who inspired us with their questioning faith. We were touched by the images and experiences of God they shared with us.

This book is an effort to combine many lived experiences of God. For each of us the encounter with God is deeply personal, yet there are recurring themes among the various contributions. Nature, love, suffering and serving the poor are all mirrors to the divine. *Where I Find God* is a collection of images, reflections and sacred moments from a wide variety of Irish people. Some of the contributions are from people we met on the road as we gave talks. Others you may recognise for being very successful in their own field.

Words on their own are inadequate when trying to describe God, for that reason we asked four photographers to donate images to complement the written contributions. The images stir in us an appreciation for the handiwork of God.

Jesus always looked out for the most vulnerable in society and in compiling this book we felt we should too. The homeless crisis in Ireland is at an all-time high. We see families, young children, teenagers, people of all ages and backgrounds without a place to call home. Many sleep rough on the streets of our towns and cities, some in crisis accommodation while others go in search of a hostel each evening. Homeless people have nowhere to call home; most do not know where their next meal, shower or quiet moment will come from. All the royalties from the sale of *Where I Find God* will be shared between Focus Ireland and the Peter McVerry Trust. Many of the contributors and photographers who so generously gave of their time and energy did so, hoping to make some small difference to those who are homeless.

Where I Find God is the kind of book that you can delve into at regular intervals. We hope this book allows you to slow down a little, find some quiet time and the opportunity to reflect on where you find God. May you the reader be blessed with an abundance of God-filled moments.

— *Cora and Joanne*

Acknowledgements

We would like to thank Patrick O'Donoghue, Helene Pertl, Ellen Monnelly, Michael Brennan and all at Columba Press for producing such a beautiful book. It is everything we dreamed it would be and more.

To Professor Mary McAleese for your profound generosity in not only contributing a piece for the book but also writing the foreword, we extend our gratitude.

To our contributors, without you there would be no book. Thank you for sharing your personal encounters with God. It is in sharing these sacred moments that others will be inspired.

To John Kelly, Norman McCloskey, Christy McNamara and Giles Norman for your very kind support in donating the images which help capture the essence of *Where I Find God*.

And finally to our husbands, Cathal Boyce and Declan Hogan, for being our rocks and always supporting us. Thanks for recording us for YouTube, tolerating our late-night meetings and for ferrying us to and from those meetings on occasion.

Image © Norman McCloskey

Image © Norman McCloskey

Cora Guinnane

As I contemplate and reflect on where I find God, there is no one place or time that I associate as being the place where I encounter God. However, there are some occasions when I feel God's presence even more so in my life. The sense of peace and acceptance in my heart during difficult times in life assures me that God is present. I have a deep conviction that God has a plan for me and my family. During the most difficult of times and despite being upset or disappointed, I have a strong sense that all will be well; God has a plan! I am very aware of God's presence when I take time out to sit on the wall in Lahinch and reflect on all that is going on in my life, when I am driving to Dublin with only the radio for company, when I pop into the church on my way to or from the shop just to have a quick chat with God. I see and feel God when the tiny hands of my daughter wrap around my neck, and at night when I stand by my daughters' beds and marvel at their perfection. These sacred moments remind me that the miracle of life is so precious.

Joanne O'Brien

I see God as the architect of the universe and God's spirit, therefore, is present in all of creation. On my drive to work, I pass through an area aptly named Paradise, where a winding road meanders through an area of vast beauty. Beech trees tower and drape over beautifully built stone walls and I'm reminded of the creator every time I pass through. I continue to look for God's spirit throughout the day: in each and every person I encounter at work; in listening to the words of wisdom that come from my children; in the love and kindness of my husband; in the goodness of my parents.

I see God at work when I look back upon a period in my life that was challenging, and I begin to understand what God was up to, pushing me (sometimes gently, sometimes not) to become more, to grow more. I am deeply nourished when I connect with the divine within. 'For in him we live and move and have our being', Acts 17:28. When I slow down and enter silence, I discover the sacred space of the soul, where God speaks, and it is here where the worries and concerns melt away.

2

Harry Bohan

I'm a priest in a busy parish, a population of approximately 6,000. For a number of years now I have been almost consumed by ministry. Time off is not a priority for me. I tend to find my energy within the parish, being involved in different pastoral and spiritual initiatives there. I also tend to find God in this, and especially in the way I try to pray the Mass and connect the sacraments to people on special occasions for them: such as baptism, marriage, first communion, confirmation, sacrament of reconciliation, anointing. Preparation for these is important to me, as is preaching, visiting the sick and so on. I believe deeply in trying to connect the Christian message and the Word of God to the reality of people's lives – in word and in practice.

I also believe in the concept of community, and I see the parish as a Christian community which at times might involve me in a range of practical initiatives to enhance the life of the community.

All of this might sound great. And I do find God there. However, I realise now, and have realised for some time, that I need to develop a discipline of prayer which would hopefully lead to being at home with God – finding time 'to be' in His presence. I deeply believe God reveals His plans to us through the Word, and in sending us His Son He has made known His plans for the world.

Every day at Mass I realise the importance of 'breaking the Word' for myself and the people. Often, in trying to meaningfully express the Word for the people, I find a richness in it myself.

Again, however, I struggle with my faith, and with allowing Jesus to have a central place in my life. So much of what I believe is a mystery and I accept that. Connecting with Inner Self, Others, Creation, and the Creator is probably a good definition of spirituality and the spiritual journey, but I have a long way to go on that journey. In short, I am very aware that I am so caught up with my pastoral work and other people's problems, that I have neglected my need to spend more time in a personal relationship with God.

Harry Bohan grew up in Feakle, Co. Clare and was ordained for the Killaloe diocese in 1963. After ordination he studied sociology. He is renowned for his work in the areas of rural housing and community development and is the founder of the Céifin conference for values-led change. He is also a former manager of the Clare hurling team. His autobiography, *Swimming Upstream*, was published in 2013. He is currently parish priest in Sixmilebridge, Co. Clare.

Image © Christy McNamara

4

Harry Brady

When first asked this question I had to stop and wonder how to answer. The first thing that came to mind was what I learnt as a child: God is everywhere. It was an answer trotted out without thought or understanding.

The prayer 'Our Father who art in Heaven' came to mind. Jesus set aside time for prayer, keeping alive his relationship with God his father. He wanted us, his followers, to pray also. The Lord's Prayer was a model for us. It is not easy to pray or to set aside time for prayer in a busy world. We can become too familiar with the words, and undervalue them. St Augustine said, 'If we turn to God it is a gift in itself.'

The picture of God as a living father is predominant in the New Testament. Jesus prayed to God his father. He is the perfect father caring for his children, 'Holy God.' He is found in sacred places – thy kingdom come. If He is everywhere He can be found where I work or play, land or seas, home or abroad.

My work should be an act of love if love will use the gifts God gave me – 'thy will be done'. He can be found in pain and suffering as we reflect on what life is: 'They that are healthy have no need of the physician but they that are ill.' Pain can focus the mind. We all need help sometimes. Our Lord knows that and surely will pity us.

Made in the image and likeness of God, each person can tell us something about God which nobody else can; they can say something only they can say.

Our faith reveals the truth about God and the truth about ourselves and as St Irenaeus said: 'The Glory of God is in the human person fully alive.'

Harry Brady was born on 7 January 1938 in Scariff, Co. Clare. He attended Scariff National School and St Flannan's College, Ennis. He was ordained in the Cathedral of the Assumption, Carlow on 8 June 1963 for the Killaloe diocese. He served the people in the parish of Clarecastle Ballyea faithfully as parish priest and, since September 2014, now acts as assistant priest.

Image © Norman McCloskey

Fr Paddy Byrne S.M.

Where do I find God? Maybe it's God who finds us. If you look at the Bible, God makes the initial approach; it is God who finds us. If you go right back to Adam, God calls out 'Where are you?' It is God who calls Abraham and also Moses. Jonah tried to get away from God, but he didn't in the end.

We must look for divine presence – what is God saying to me here? God is always at work. We are expected to see signs of God. Sometimes God challenges us to do things we don't want. We don't like to change our thinking, but God wants us to. God is always at work.

I have to face the Creator, and what's he going to say to me? I've been very fortunate to have come from a good home and I have had a five-star education. I like to think that I've helped people, that all I have been given is to help others, not to stick feathers in my own cap. I began my education with the Mercy nuns and then continued on with the Marists for ten years, after which I did a degree in English in UCD; it was while I was in UCD that the supernatural or grace came in. I decided to give the priesthood a go and see what happened. I felt at home as a Marist priest. I always experienced love and encouragement at home and when I decided to enter the priesthood my mother encouraged me to go and also reminded me that if it didn't work out I could return home. 'This is where you belong,' she said.

I studied philosophy in UCD and then I was sent to Rome to study theology, and I lectured in the seminary for a while. I studied a course in Pentateuch and it was at this point where I became really interested in scripture. I spent three years lecturing and studying scripture in Jerusalem. The Lord sent me on a path – I wondered what for, but delighted in helping others. If I wouldn't help then I shouldn't be ordained. Over the years I found my students very charitable. There were always signs of God's presence in what I was doing. God is always at work!

Fr Paddy Byrne S.M. is a biblical scholar and theologian. He grew up in Dundalk and was ordained as a Marist priest in 1956. He has lectured in Rome, Jerusalem, New Zealand, Australia, Fiji and Papua New Guinea and has spent almost forty years lecturing in the Milltown Institute, Dublin. At eighty-six years of age, he spends his days in the library of the Milltown Institute, reading the books he only had time to reference while he was a full-time lecturer.

Image © Giles Norman

Jerry Carey

I grew to believe that I meet God, potentially, in every person and in every event. Along the way I have had my truly epiphanic moments when deeply I knew that God had woken me to His presence.

My parents taught me how to begin my day and end my day with a conscious God-meeting moment; today I continue this ritual.

Some people have blessed my journey with their witness to God's presence, causing me to pause and think, to look and to find. Some through their quiet serenity, some through their belief that God brought them through potential despair and defeat.

Then, I stumbled upon Taizé, a community in France which welcomes young people to share their 'Parable of Communion'. A communion shared with many more, with God at the heart of everything we do there.

I like to call God 'The Creator God'. I experience that 'Wonder and Awe in God's Presence' early on a spring/summer morning, when the fallow time of winter is replaced with the vibrant greening of nature's resurrection.

I continue to search for God in every person and in every event.

Jerry Carey is fifty-five years of age and is thirty-two years in ministry. He is chaplain to Coláiste Muire Secondary School, Ennis and has mainly served in three parishes: Clarecastle, Ennis and now, as parish priest, Doora–Barefield. He has been bringing groups of young people to Taizé in France since 1990, where he shares with thousands of young people from all over Europe what is beautiful about faith, culture and life; this he believes is probably the most rewarding element of his experience in ministry.

Image © Norman McCloskey

Roger Childs

The world is charged with the grandeur of God.
It will flame out, like shining from shook foil.

When saying where he found God, Gerard Manley Hopkins went for the easy option: the splendour of nature. It's much harder to find God in nature's less splendid, even grisly and cruel, aspects: a tsunami or, as Stephen Fry recently suggested to Gay Byrne on RTÉ's *The Meaning of Life*, 'bone cancer in children'. It's the age-old challenge of theodicy: why would a good God let bad stuff happen? Elijah found God not in the tempest, the fire or the earthquake, but in the whispering breeze that followed. And yet logic tells us that God must be in all of those things, or none.

Hardest of all, perhaps, is to find God in the place where we would least expect to find him: in ourselves. Is there a way of giving meaning to the notion that we are created in God's image without accidentally recreating God in *our* image instead? The prophet Micah's tip for finding and revealing God in the best of ourselves was to 'act justly, love mercy and walk humbly'. My own version of that is 'the three hums': *hum*ility, *hum*anity and *hum*our (and no *hum*bug!). Better still, follow the even simpler signpost offered by Jesus and The Beatles: 'All you need is love.'

Roger Childs is RTÉ's Senior Production Executive and head of RTÉ religious programmes. A Cambridge English graduate and multi-award-winning producer, he worked at WNET, New York, Channel 4 and the BBC, before joining RTÉ in 2007. He is responsible for a broad range of religious content across all media, including *The Meaning of Life*, with Gay Byrne, *Would You Believe?*, and a rich variety of commissioned output, such as *One Million Dubliners*, *Baz: The Lost Muslim* and *Mary McAleese and The Man Who Saved Europe*.

Image © John Kelly

Dr Finola Cunnane

As a child, God was an awesome, majestic and powerful God. I recall finding God in the beautiful sunsets I admired from my parents' bedroom window; when playing in the brilliant sunshine; and while watching the rainstorms, thunderstorms and snowstorms.

As an adolescent, I found God in my yearning and dreaming, in my desires to change the world, to make a difference. I specifically recall meeting God through those who awakened and stirred these longings within me.

As a young adult, I found God through study and my rapidly expanding horizons and possibilities. I found God in mission, in a sense of purpose, in the challenges and particularly in and through the people with whom I lived and worked.

While I still find God in all of the above, I am now aware of a God located deep within my being. This is the God whose presence I experience in the quiet, silent moments of deeper breathing, in the growing awareness of living meaningfully and purposefully and through the frequent glimpses that reveal more of who I am and who God is. This is the God who helps me recognise the God in others and in the various dimensions of our inner and outer journeys.

Dr Finola Cunnane holds a Ph.D in Education and Leadership from Fordham University, New York. She has lectured extensively in Education, Spirituality, Theology, Psychology and Pastoral Care throughout Ireland, Europe, Canada, USA, West Africa and New Zealand. Belonging to the Sisters of St Louis, Finola is author of *New Directions in Religious Education*, as well as over one hundred articles.

Image © Giles Norman

Eleanor Custy

Finding God is sometimes a very difficult thing to do in a world where there are daily disasters, terror attacks and death, especially for a young person; where there are people who don't have a home or a family or anywhere they can feel safe. It is difficult to find God in a world that feels so unequal and wrong.

I was always a religious person, but as I started to grow up and was trying to find myself in the world I started to lose Him a little bit. I think it was my ego: I was edging God out. I still went to Mass, I still believed, but I stopped looking for Him. It was around then that I went to Calcutta doing voluntary work for the Missionaries of Charity. It was there I saw true poverty and the hardship of life and it was there that I found God. I found Him in the work my classmates and I were doing; I found Him in the eyes of the beautiful street kids; and I found Him in the sheer happiness that surrounded me. When I came home I decided I wanted to make more of an impact and to help other young people just like me struggling to find God.

At home I find God in the amazing work the Youth Council do; I find him in their enthusiasm and their dedication. I find God when I succeed in life and when things go my way, but more importantly I find Him when things don't go my way, because I know for sure that once I have found Him he is never going to give up on me.

Eleanor Custy is a nineteen-year-old student of International Development and Food Policy in UCC. She lives in Doora–Barefield, Co. Clare and is an active member of her parish. She is the current chairperson of the Killaloe Diocesan Youth Council and has helped to organise many youth events throughout the diocese. She also partakes in charity work and this year travelled to Calcutta, India to work as a volunteer with the Hope Foundation for six weeks.

Image © John Kelly

Fr Pádraig J. Daly

Often when I look for God, I do not find God. But sometimes I stumble upon Him/Her/ The Other unexpectedly: when sun shines, when rains fall, when a bird sings, when the vastness of the universe overwhelms me, when I am listening to impossible grief. The initiative, I believe, is God's, not mine. The poem below speaks of one moment of awareness of God:

PLACE

Sitting before a great cathedral,
Letting my eye move up along the stone
In the last of the sunlight,
Watching pigeons find their niches,
Small birds drop for crumbs,
A dog twist, lazy-bellied, on the steps,
I am certain still
That every drifting mote has place;
And we are gathered all
In the upswell of Benevolence.

Fr Pádraig J. Daly is a contemporary Irish poet. He was born near Dungarvan, Co. Waterford and is now working as an Augustinian priest in Dublin, serving as parish priest in Ballyboden. He has published several collections of poetry, among them *The Last Dreamers: New & Selected Poems* and *The Other Sea*.

Image © Giles Norman

Fr Brian D'Arcy C.P.

I am blessed to live in a stunningly beautiful place. So when God is absent, I take a boat to one of Lough Erne's many unspoilt islands.

In May, Inish Davar, an uninhabited island of about ten acres in the middle of Lower Lough Erne, becomes a rich, swaying carpet of dazzling bluebells.

A few days ago I was stunned by a magnificent, uplifting vision of nature.

There were daisies, proud white May flowers, and sturdy ancient trees of every kind. Thorn bushes were in bloom; there was a choir of birdsong; and to cap it all, I stood in awe at the cuckoo's friendly call. Lough Erne's water was as calm as a pond.

My spirits were consumed by the stillness of this heaven on earth. No matter how bad life appears to be, God is all around me here if I open my eyes and ears to God's many voices.

Joyce Kilmer's poem, 'Trees', comes to mind:

I think that I shall never see
A poem lovely as a tree …

A tree that looks at God all day …

Poems are made by fools like me
But only God can make a tree.

Fr Brian D'Arcy is a Passionist priest based at the Graan Monastery near Enniskillen, Co. Fermanagh, Northern Ireland. He is one of the best known and most popular priests in Ireland. He is a noted author, newspaper columnist, broadcaster and preacher.

Image © Norman McCloskey

Dr Ronnie Delany

I am happy to share with you how my religious faith helped me to realise my potential as a person and an athlete.

When I was a pupil at Catholic University School, a Marist college in Dublin, I was interested in many sports. C.U.S. is a comparatively small school and it was possible for me to gain selection on a number of teams. At this impressionable age I was very much influenced by my mentors. I did not realise then the importance the Marist teaching and tradition would play in my future sports career.

I was taught to desire to win, but I was not led into the fool's paradise of believing success would come without effort. While encouraged to enjoy victory, we were advised to be modest and considerate of the feelings of our opponents. We learnt to share victory and defeat in the proper manner.

After school I enrolled at Villanova University, near Philadelphia, run by the Augustinian Fathers. For the next five years my life was a routine of lectures, studying, training under Jumbo Elliot, a legendary coach, and racing practically every week, throughout the United States and later all over the world.

At that time I was scrupulously religious. I found that the tension of participating internationally at the highest competitive level brought me closer to God, an experience that I believe is shared by many athletes across the spectrum of sport.

A greater responsibility now falls on the athlete to perform to a standard of moral conduct equal to the sporting achievement. Fair play, mutual respect and friendship should be the goals of sport at all levels. Sportsmen and sportswomen can show the youth of the world how to play the game – both on and off the field – and so contribute to the truest form of education: that of human character.

I achieved my lifetime ambition in winning an Olympic Gold medal for Ireland. I can recall my emotions at the finish of an epic 1,500 metres final. My heart swelled with joy as I approached the finish line. I threw my arms out wide in exultation as I broke the tape and dropped to my knees in a prayer of thanksgiving. This was instinctive, such was my faith, my recognition of my God-given talent. It was my destiny to win the most sought-after gold medal in the world of sport.

Ronnie Delany is a former Irish athlete who specialised in middle-distance running. He won a gold medal in the 1,500 metres at the 1956 Olympics in Melbourne. Delany's US running career is legendary: from 1955 through 1959 he ran forty races undefeated indoors, setting the world record for the mile three times. He is one of the greatest sportsmen and international ambassadors in his country's history.

Image © Norman McCloskey

Joe Duffy

[I find God in moments, like the one I photographed for this card.]

Liveline RTÉ Radio
I.V. MMXXV

Dear Cara + Joanne —
I find God in moments
like the one I photographed
for this card.
Thks + Best wishs with the project
Joe Duffy

Joe Duffy presents one of Ireland's leading radio shows, *Liveline*, on RTÉ Radio One. *Liveline*, which has 400,000 listeners, is now firmly established as a national institution, as listeners tune and call in to the show to 'Talk to Joe.'

In 2015, Joe brought *Liveline* to our TV screens with *Liveline: Call Back*. In this show, Joe looked back at some of the standout stories, some with heartbreaking and others with heart-warming outcomes. He also presents *Joe Duffy's Spirit Level* on RTÉ One.

Joe released his award-winning and bestselling book, *Children of the Rising*, with Hachette in 2015. This is the first ever account of the young lives violently lost during the week of the 1916 Rising: long-forgotten and never commemorated, until now. Previously he released his autobiography *Just Joe* in 2011. He also writes for the *Mail on Sunday*.

Fr Gerard Fitzgerald

As the dawn breaks into a beautiful sunrise, the dew glistens on the grass and spiders' webs, and the earth hangs in a delicate balance between night and day, there is God. In the illumination of the sun, lavishing upon us the balm of life-giving warmth, there is God. When I wake in the morning, and recognise that I am not what I ought, want or even hope to be, but that by the grace of God I am what I am, there is God. There is God, coaxing and encouraging me, as gently as the sun encourages the flowers to open their heads. Why? Because God loves me; and nothing that I can do will change that. He desires that I grow into the best version of myself.

In times of joy, in times of hope, there is God. There is the God who can change water into wine (Jn 2:1–12), mourning into dancing (Ps 30:11), the God 'who has anointed me to bring good news to the afflicted; to bind up the broken-hearted, to proclaim liberty to captives and freedom to prisoners; to proclaim the favourable year of the Lord' (Isa 61:1–3). God wants us to be happy and our human hearts yearn for that happiness; therein lies the genius of Christianity. However, it is only when we lift our heads to the light of God in Christ and allow him to burn up our sinfulness, frailties and brokenness, that we can blossom as God wants us to. That is why the Year of Mercy is so important: it acknowledges our need for forgiveness, but it also recognises the magnificent treasure that we are. God wishes us to experience his mercy and will go to the greatest of lengths to achieve this.

I find God in the love of others, both given and received; in the beauty of the created world; in the most unlikely of places. In this Year of Mercy, look for God, remembering, in the words of a famous proverb by Elif Shafak: 'How we see God is a direct reflection of how we see ourselves. If God brings to mind mostly fear and blame, it means there is too much fear and blame welled inside us. If we see God as full of love and compassion, so are we.' Allow the sun to shine, because there is God.

Fr Gerard Fitzgerald is a priest of the parish of Ennis in the diocese of Killaloe. He was born in Castleconnell in Co. Limerick and studied for the priesthood in Maynooth between 2005–2011. He is interested in social justice issues, Law (especially Criminal, Tort and Contract), studying the scriptures and dogma. He lists Pope Francis, Oscar Romero and Justice Antonin Scalia among his influences.

Image © John Kelly

Tommy Fleming

I suppose you could say the easy answer to this is 'God is everywhere'. To explain a little more, this is my opinion, and to fully explain you must also understand that I wouldn't consider myself to be overly religious in any way. But I do believe there is good and evil and sometimes in this complex world of ours these get mixed up and cause disruption to our daily lives and understanding.

When I say God is everywhere I believe God is in nature with the bursting of life that spring brings; it can brighten your mood and offer peace and well-being. This is God.

I believe God is in humanity and compassion, when you see reactions to natural disasters across the world and the generosity of people with their time, donations and all types of help that humanity offers to others.

Kindness in others is one of the finest examples of where God is. It carries across all communities worldwide and, from the smallest gesture of goodwill to the sacrifice of some for the benefit of others, this is where I see God.

Kindness is not limited to humans, and to me the return of unconditional love from animals is one of the biggest influences on when we find God.

Tommy Fleming is one of Ireland's finest solo singers, with a hugely successful international singing career. On 30 March 2012, Tommy lost both his parents, a tragedy that inspired both his autobiography and the recording of the album *Begin*, which Tommy describes as the most 'cathartic work he has ever done and a fitting and personal tribute to his beloved Mother and Father'.

Image © Norman McCloskey

Finbar Furey

I've slept rough on the streets of my home city of Dublin and a few other streets on my travels many years ago, and it is the most degrading, unworthy place to rest your mind, body or soul. It's not nice to wake up cold and damp, shivering to keep calm and stay focussed on keeping yourself warm if at all possible. Often it isn't, until the sun shines again. If it does, you're blessed.

Prayer enters your hopes and somehow or other it makes you more determined to step out to a better place, better times and life. But is anyone listening?

ANNABEL

I sat and I talked with old Annabel
Some say she's crazy, quite insane.
But she offered me wine
The only time her life feels real
It's when she's drinking, dreaming when she can
She wants to die in those arms.
She's older now than freedom's seen
So cold, so lonely and tired or begging, please.
She falls down on her knees
Her heart unfold to repeal her soul
She screams at me: 'There's no god you know!'
I know.
I can tell you so.
For this god I know.
For this god I know.

Finbar Furey is a multi-instrumental folk musician. He is best known for his band of brothers, The Fureys. He is a renowned musician, songwriter, producer and actor.

Image © Giles Norman

Sr Mary Bonaventure Greene

In Jesus! I find God in the words and actions of Jesus: in His personal approach towards others, His gentleness, His compassion. I find God when I walk the Way of the Cross, witnessing the love that gave everything; the love of Jesus who forgave even those who crucified Him.

I believe Jesus is alive today as truly as He was alive two thousand years ago. I encounter Him every time I witness or experience kindness, forgiveness, genuine friendship, human togetherness. I discover Him in those who suffer; in those who accompany a suffering sister or brother. I encounter the Spirit of God when true peace takes hold of the heart; when those who have hurt one another embrace and continue the journey of life together. I find God when I join together with others to do good. Joy wells up within. I experience God when, faced with my own weakness over and over again, I pray: 'Lord, you know everything, you know that I love you.' Jesus is the most faithful friend you or I will ever find.

Sr Bonaventure Greene was born in Ennis on 5 June 1959. She was educated at Holy Family Primary School and Coláiste Mhuire, Ennis. She entered the Poor Clare Monastery in Galway city following one year's study in NUIG. She spent ten years in a Poor Clare Monastery in Nigeria, returning to the Galway monastery in July 2009.

Image © Norman McCloskey

Roseanne Healy

Where do I find God? As a mother.

Children love to laugh and play, mix and socialise, engage and exchange games and ideas with other children regardless of race, religious background, skin colour or socio-economic group. Children provide a security zone and comfort for each other.

I find God in children when they mix freely with other children without any preconceived or preformed prejudices. I see God when they console each other and help each other when needed.

In his parables and miracles Jesus did not judge or offer help to only one group in society. He cured the sick and the lame and forgave sinners, showing us that the kingdom of God is open freely to all.

While having a sense of gratitude for the luxuries we enjoy in my home, I hope my children will develop an awareness of the needs of other children, which are not always met by society.

Roseanne Healy is married to Donie and has two children, Aoife and Donnchadh. She grew up near Castlecomer, Co. Kilkenny. She teaches in the Christian Brothers Secondary School, Ennistymon, Co. Clare. Roseanne has found her calling in passing on the faith in a creative way to the young people in the children's liturgy in the friary in Ennis.

Image © John Kelly

34

Des Hillery

At the time of writing, the people of Nepal are struggling. Nepal is a country which is home to millions and which is the destination of countless visitors because of its natural beauty and culture. Today it is shattered. An earthquake of 7.9 on the Richter scale has thrown up the cry: 'Why did God allow this to happen?' The cry of the poor.

On 15 August 2007 at 6.40 p.m. an earthquake of 7.9 devastated the central coast of Peru. I can recall vividly where I was, whom I was with and the exact time it occurred. I was in Lima and felt the earth shake and heard the noise of destruction, even though I was over 150 km from the epicentre. I travelled south to Ica, the region affected by the earthquake, and saw for myself the destruction. I also witnessed the immense goodness and mercy of people.

In one section of Ica lived a community of Columban Missionary sisters, some of whom are Irish. They worked as the conduits of kindness, receiving the generosity of the Irish, planning with the local population their response to the earthquake and attempting to meet the needs of those grappling to survive; basic needs such as water, food, shelter, medicines and security. Sprouting from the rubble crept huts that were assembled with material funded out of generosity. Homes were created by the local families and a community springing up with an undying spirit.

'Where do I find God?' you ask. I find God not in the abstract philosophical or theological answers, but rather in the heart of each person. Because God hears the cry of the poor.

Des Hillery is from Miltown Malbay, Co. Clare and is currently parish priest of Nenagh, Co. Tipperary. Previous appointments were as a member of the teaching staff of St Flannan's College, Ennis, of the formation team of St Patrick's College, Maynooth and as an associate with the Columban Missionaries in Peru. Des is also now acting as the administrator of the diocese of Killaloe.

Image © Christy McNamara

Colm Hogan

'Where do I find God?' has to be one of the most thought-provoking questions that anyone can ask themselves throughout life, whether you believe in a God or not.

Where I find God is the place where I find hope, inspiration, love and wholeness. I am fortunate that I find this God in many places in my life, including my home, my family and friends, and my work colleagues.

Below is an experience from a recent trip to Uganda in my capacity as Church Outreach Officer with Trócaire.

I remember seeing Daniel's face on the Trócaire box in 2012 and wondering what life must be like in his village in northern Uganda; imagine my amazement in January 2016, when I found myself standing with Daniel in his home village of Barlonyo.

It was a great privilege to meet the young boy whose face already seemed so familiar to me. Since his story featured on the Trócaire box, Daniel has continued his schooling and now attends a primary boarding school in nearby Lira. And he still wants to be a doctor, as was his wish in 2012.

We sat with Daniel and his family and heard his mother, Betty, say how proud she is of her son. Emmanuel, who is Daniel's older brother, is also studying and wants to become a nurse. He entertained us with a song of welcome which spoke of Trócaire's help to his family. It was a deeply touching moment.

Whilst emphasising that meeting Daniel strongly affirmed for me that we can find God in people, I should point out that one does not have to travel to find God; the challenge is to acknowledge God's presence in the humble living out of daily life.

Colm Hogan works with Trócaire, the overseas agency of the Irish Catholic Church, in the role of Church Outreach Officer. He works with laity and clergy in parishes throughout Ireland delivering on Trócaire's message of justice for all.

Image © Norman McCloskey

Sr Carmel Kehoe

From New Ross, on a fair day, my father always returned home with a packet of Rolos for me. Sweets, in the heart of the country, were a rare commodity. At a very young age I had heard about 'miracles'. When I received my treat I would go out to the barn, put the sweets on my tiny hand, and pray fervently to God. My eyes would open in wonder as I longingly hoped the sweets would increase. That was my first encounter with the notion of miracle!

Where do I find God today? I know that God is love. Out of love He has created us humans and all living things. For me, everything is permeated by love and God is present in all things.

When major catastrophes occur my faith in God is challenged. Where is the loving God now, I wonder. No matter how I struggle I come back to knowing that God lives only as love – even in pain and suffering – and He is there when we call on Him to comfort and console.

When I pray I like to meditate. This helps me journey to that still point which is the God-centre within me. It is here that I can travel gently to

> That place where I can recover
> My core of silence
> To find again my soul's delight
> To feel the embrace of God.

Carmel Kehoe was born in Lacken, near New Ross, Co. Wexford. She is a sister of St John of God. She spent a number of years working as Hospital Chaplain in Daisy Hill, Newry and Beaumont Hospital, Dublin. She spent the years before her retirement working as a special needs teacher in schools in Clare. She has published many short stories and poems.

Image © John Kelly

Cathy Kelly

For so long God was sold to us as a deity who dealt out fire and brimstone and who judged fiercely, with a ledger of misdemeanours to be ticked off. I could never identify with that God. Instead, I could see God, or a Higher Power or Divinity, in kind people who cared about the world, who'd take care of the small children hungry for food and water, who'd bring soup and a kind word to the person in the doorway when everyone else turned away.

Eventually, I realised that this spirituality I believed in was faith in the inherent goodness of humankind, the belief that God was in people, not in rules or regulations or buildings.

So now I find God in the everyday. We have that divinity in us and we can make choices to help our fellow human beings. Nobody needs to tell us, it is in our hearts and souls, whether we've heard of God before or not.

That God is the spirit of kindness in a human being who gives a lift to the person who has no car when the bus is late and the rain is falling like needles.

That God is the tireless charity worker who tries to raise the money so that even one child can be saved from death due to drinking dirty water.

That God is the friend who listens to another person's pain and offers them kind words.

That God doesn't care what religion or race you are.

That God, that kindness, is in all individuals who help people who, for a myriad of reasons, cannot help themselves.

That God tries to understand the complex series of events that leads a person to lie in that huddle of blankets, scared, lonely, and hungry, seemingly invisible to the people who think the blankets and the doorway are a choice when they are actually the result of having no choice left.

The kindness to help and not to judge is where I find God.

Cathy Kelly is a former journalist and now full-time writer who is published around the world, with millions of books in print in many languages. She lives with her husband, twin sons and three dogs in Co. Wicklow in Ireland. She is also a Goodwill Ambassador for UNICEF Ireland, raising funds and awareness for UNICEF's amazing work.

Image © John Kelly

Friar Liam Kelly

In a wooden frame placed inside the door of the Franciscan Novitiate House in Chilworth, near Guilford in England, was a quaint, hand-painted image of a field mouse almost buried amidst leaves and ferns and moss. The little mouse peeks through the woodland floor and circling the image, in beautiful calligraphy, are the words: 'To Seek God, you must first of all allow yourself to be found by Him.'

Where do I find God? I don't really seek God like an explorer or a scientist. Rather, God finds me, surprises me and searches me; that is the dynamic of faith. It is God who invites and God who seeks. I can identify with the field mouse, who emerges from the camouflage of the woodland floor, so as to be found, to be known and ultimately to be in the presence of God.

My Christian faith, based on the incarnation of the Word of God, Jesus, helps me to seek God in the world around me and the people whose paths I cross each day. I must expect to find God there. I find God in the lives of others, in the sacraments, in prayer and in the scriptures. But mostly, God finds me.

A native of Glinsk in Co. Galway, Liam Kelly OFM entered the Franciscan Order in 1995. Since ordination to the priesthood in 2005 he has worked in pastoral ministry in Killarney, Ennis and Athlone, and in secondary school chaplaincy in Killarney, Ennis, Ennistymon, Gormanston College and recently in Athlone. He feels blessed in recent years to work with other friars in leading parish missions here in Ireland and to be involved in retreat work. He is currently Assistant Director of Formation in Athlone.

Image © John Kelly

Maureen Kelly

I am often more aware of restlessness than stillness. Living in the fast lane, I find myself out of touch with presence or a sense of the divine.

When I am out of touch like this, I love to visit the ancient holy places. They reconnect me to my own heart's prayer, to God, to stillness, to the generations who have visited these sacred places before me. One of my favourites is Scattery Island, *Inis Cathaigh*, off the coast of Clare. To this solitary island at the mouth of the Shannon, the great Senan came, after a lifetime of journeying in far-away places. To be here is to be filled with questions: what deep searching brought him here?

'Let your feet follow your heart until you find your place of resurrection.' So ran the proverb of the ancient Celtic monks. It evokes their prayer that they might find the place of risen life, and know Christ's risen presence, against the pull of everything that would limit and keep their vision small. For Senan, this secluded island was his place of resurrection.

On Scattery, I am put in touch with my heart's longing for that risen presence and am moved to make that prayer myself.

Maureen Kelly is a lay pastoral worker with the Killaloe diocese working in the area of liturgy and spirituality. She is particularly interested in new expressions of spirituality and in how we can engage with the hunger for depth and meaning in today's culture. A native of Clare, she has a specific love for ancient holy places and leads pilgrim walks to monastic sites and holy wells associated with the Celtic Church.

Image © John Kelly

Sr Stanislaus Kennedy

I like to think of my life as a journey, a journey from God to God. But actually, there are two journeys: an outward and an inward. My outward journey was into education, work, ministry and service. That journey took me from Dingle to Dublin, to Kilkenny and back to Dublin; from home, to school, to the novitiate; and to the service of the poor, in Kilkenny Social Services, Focus Ireland, the Immigrant Council of Ireland, the Young Social Innovators and the Sanctuary. In each place I have found God, especially in the poor, vulnerable and marginalised people I encountered on my journey.

The second journey is an inward journey. That is the journey into my true self, the *I am*, the God within me and around me; that is my journey into prayer and meditation and towards my ultimate home in God. These two journeys are of course closely intertwined. They interact with and affect each other all the time. And so it is that when I come to describe the inward journey of the soul, I begin always from my involvement with the poor. The poor are, and have been, a source of life and healing to me every day of my life. As I walk with them, I have begun to understand better Jesus' relationship with the poor of his time. He said 'Blessed are the poor in spirit', and his whole life demonstrates his love for the poor and his belief that those who were rejected by society are blessed.

Throughout my life, God has also spoken to me through my weakness. Through the cracks in my life, when I was open to it, God's radiance shone. Life taught this to me: the more I surrendered, the more I was able to let go of false images of myself, and see and accept myself as I really was: vulnerable, weak, afraid, anxious. And once I began to accept this, I began also to realise that God wanted to meet me there, in my brokenness, and that I could only really let God in through those broken parts of me. This was not something I could have done by myself; it only happens when I let God take over. And that is how it is that the radiance of God lights my way and leads me safely down the road home.

Sr Stanislaus Kennedy, 'Sr Stan', is a well-known social campaigner and founder of a number of voluntary organisations, including Focus Ireland, the Immigrant Council of Ireland, Young Social Innovators and the Sanctuary. She has received numerous awards and tributes in Ireland and elsewhere for her outstanding work for the marginalised in society. She is the author of several bestselling books, including *To Live from the Heart, Seasons of Hope, Day by Day, The Road Home* and *Moments of Stillness*.

Image © Norman McCloskey

SPLINTERS

Through frenzy, chaos, desire and distress
In the infinitesimal space
Between one shuddering breath
And the next,
I exhale.
Aeons of tears and of secrets and of songs,
The poet whose voice is never heard,
The weeping mother without her child,
The rotting fools who thought their reign
Would never end
I exhale.
Transient splinters of sights and tastes and sounds,
That for one tantalising second
In the cold mist of dawn,
Come together to make story.

Mary Kennelly

When you can see God in small things, you'll see God in all things.
— Donald L. Hicks, *Look into the Stillness*

A few years ago I changed jobs, having worked for years for the Department of Education. I liked my job supporting schools and teachers throughout the country but I knew it was time for a change. I took a job in Ennistymon, Co. Clare. I like my job, it's a privilege to work in a secondary school, and there is an energy around young people that is unlike anything else. So far so understandable. The thing that drew most comment from people I talked to however was not that I changed from one job to the other but that I worked in Ennistymon while living in Glin, Co. Limerick. This left me commuting for roughly three hours every day. To most this seemed like madness, I know this because they told me so.

I had a slightly different take on the matter. Whilst enjoyable and fulfilling, mine was a job that could draw you in, cause you to lose sleep and tie you up in knots. For me the stillness of the journey to and from work allowed me time to take up or lay down the thousand individual things that made up my daily work. It meant when I went home, I could be at home fully and when I was at work I was ready for the day. No matter what was on my mind when I sat into the car, the length of the journey meant that I had time to process, to plan and to move on from. Eventually silence came and with it an ability to look around, to see. On my way home I had the Atlantic for company, reminding me that I am only passing through, my worries are passing also. The ocean was there long before me, it will remain long after I am lost, even to memory. In the early morning I had the mist, to me it feels like the earth is exhaling before it draws in its breath to begin the frantic day.

The quietness of my morning drive, although shorter now, steadies me, allows me to see beyond myself, to find room in my head and my heart for more than myself. In the stillness I find God and in doing so I can take my God with me through the hubbub of the rest of the day.

Originally from Co. Kerry and now living in Limerick, Mary Kennelly has been involved in arts events for many years, including Listowel Writers' Week, the Brendan Kennelly Summer Festival and, as a participant, the Mindfield: Spoken Word section at Electric Picnic 2014. She has released three poetry collections: *Sunny Spells, Scattered Showers* (2004), with the artist Rebecca Carroll; *From the Stones* (2010), with the artist Brenda Fitzmaurice; and *Catching Bats Takes Patience* (2015).

Image © John Kelly

Martina Lehane Sheehan

So we are grasped by what we cannot grasp;
it has an inner light, even from a distance –

and charges us, even if we do not reach it,
into something else, which, hardly sensing it,
we already are.

— Rainer Maria Rilke, 'A Walk'

We are continually *grasped by what we cannot grasp*; when we think we have 'found' God, somehow God eludes us. Meister Eckhart, the German mystic, says 'the God we think we know is most likely not God at all'. I experience this as both frustrating and exciting, where my pilgrim heart never quite knows 'the day or the hour' when the Divine reveals itself.

Being an introvert, I tend to seek God through silence. However, sitting Zen-like and cross-legged on a cushion all day can also be an escape from difficult encounters, those who offer me that pelvic push from the womb of my little self-made cosmos.

Apparently, polished gems are created by placing the stones together into a fast-revolving barrel, where they are reshaped by cutting the corners off each other. Likewise, I discover in hindsight, when others 'cut the corners off of me' they unknowingly help me to evolve into one of those gems, which in essence *we already are*.

Martina Lehane Sheehan is a psychotherapist and spiritual guide with over twenty-five years' experience delivering workshops and retreats in Ireland and the UK. She is Director of Programmes in Ennismore Retreat Centre, Cork. She has written numerous articles and is the author of the bestselling titles *Seeing Anew: Awakening to Life's Lessons* and *Whispers in the Stillness: Mindfulness and Spirituality*. Her latest book, *Surprised by Fire*, is due for publication in spring 2017.

Image © Giles Norman

Flann Lynch (OFM Cap.)

A great breakthrough occurred for me as I pondered the meaning of the first Beatitude: 'Blessed are the poor in spirit, theirs is the kingdom of heaven.' Without meaning to, I let go and surrendered, and to my great surprise, my awareness shifted from my head to my heart. It was an experience full of love and joy, and was so all-embracing that it engaged my whole being, heart and mind, body and soul.

I discovered that, rather than trying to generate love and joy, all we need to do is to let go and surrender to what is already present. The love and joy then awaken, simply because we allow them to. And so in meditation or in quiet prayer, we are not so much doing something as allowing something to happen: God waits for us in the silence.

My moment of inspiration was life-changing, because it showed me how easy it is to meditate or pray quietly. It also got me to see others through compassionate eyes, and to see life and the future through hopeful, optimistic eyes.

I went on to explore the other Beatitudes, and found them so inspiring that I put together a spirituality programme called 'Vision', giving people an experience of the power of each of the Beatitudes. As I presented the programme to groups, we all moved together from the old, tired attitudes and language of 'I'm not good enough', to 'I'm priceless in God's eyes'; from 'It's hard' to 'It's an opportunity'; from criticising and judging to mercy and compassion, gentleness and respect, justice and peace; and from fear and worry to trust and gratitude.

The Abundance Prayer, an integral part of 'Vision', is very effective in helping us to centre our awareness in the heart. You can watch the prayer on FlannsFormation.com, where you can also find an introduction to meditation.

I know from my own experience, and that of many others, that time spent in the practice of letting go and surrendering gives rich dividends by allowing us to encounter God, because love and joy, when activated, change everything.

Flann Lynch is a Capuchin priest. He has wide experience in the field of prayer and meditation. Flann spent time in the Indian Ashram of Don Bede Griffiths, the great Benedictine mystic and writer. He also collaborated with Mother Teresa in Calcutta. Since 1995 he has been inventing and delivering an ecumenical spirituality programme called 'Vision'. He is based in Priorswood, Dublin.

Image © Norman McCloskey

Pat Malone

One of my very good friends is extremely talented on stage; she has a majestic singing voice and a wonderful stage presence. Every time I see her perform she takes my breath away. It wasn't always that way however. She is now in her mid-twenties, but I remember her first efforts to take to the stage at four or five years of age, and they were disastrous. The debut was the usual school concert at Christmas time. I can vividly remember the scene: practices done, audiences assembled, class ready, and then my friend bolting from her spot and running to the comfort of her mother's lap. It seemed then that this little one was not for the stage.

Today all is changed; she oozes confidence. How did this transformation occur? Simply because of the belief her family and friends placed in her. Thankfully they never took the advice to 'push her back on stage', or 'tell her she is letting everyone down'. No, they went the road of gentle encouragement and support, and she flourished.

Since I was ordained I have baptised hundreds, maybe even a thousand children. At the baptismal ceremony I always think of guardian angels, even though there is no mention of angels in the ceremony at all. For me they symbolise the God who journeys with us through life, and whose presence encourages, entices and supports. His presence is found in the people in our lives who, through their kindness, care and concern, allow our inner beauty to unfold and be shared with the world. I don't believe in a God who shoves us into situations and whips us into line, but one who encourages potential and helps us to fulfil our dreams. Whenever I see a human being flourishing in life, there I find God.

I was fortunate to have spent twenty-two years working in a post-primary school; for me it is the highlight of my life. I loved it, learnt a lot from it and look back proudly on that time. It is always great to meet former pupils of mine and catch up on their stories. In common with my little friend, many of them were once hesitant, shy, even afraid. When I meet them today I can truly rejoice with them, for they are flourishing, and I know I have found God.

Pat Malone is a native of Birr, Co. Offaly. He is a priest, teacher and psychotherapist. He is parish priest of Clarecastle, Co. Clare.

Image © Christy McNamara

Mary McAleese

I don't think of God in terms of a treasure hunt where I set off hoping to find Him. It usually works the other way. God finds me, often when I would rather not be found. Life would be a whole lot easier if He did not find me and nudge me awake to what I could be doing or should be doing – including believing in God. It's easy, even awe-inspiring to see and appreciate God's handiwork in my little grandson's breaking smile, or in the sweep of the buttercup meadow between my window and the silver waters of the Shannon. It's harder to look up the hill beyond the river, to where my grandparents, like so many others, once lived such frugal and sad lives; to remember the petty cruelties human beings visit upon one another, or the vainglorious evil that broke, and breaks still, so many hearts. It is in those moments that God finds me and somehow opens a space in that solid front of anger or frustration or hopelessness, a space big enough to let hope in and with it, miraculously, the energy to go again about the grace-filled things that I believe put a breaking smile on the face of God.

Mary McAleese served as the eighth President of Ireland for two terms between 1997 and 2011. Prior to this, she was appointed Professor of Criminal Law, Criminology and Penology at Trinity College Dublin in 1975, and in 1987, she returned to her alma mater, Queen's University of Belfast, to become Director of the Institute of Professional Legal Studies. She is married to Dr Martin McAleese and they have three children.

Image © Norman McCloskey

Sr Regina McHugh

We all like to *identify* God with a day that goes well, where we can speak of God's presence in terms of *blessings*. However, this perception of speaking of God alone limits our capacity to recognise His presence on our day-to-day living.

More often than not, God is found in the *overcoming*. It can come when I have to face a truth, admit a doubt, wrestle with my own limitations, lend a hand, and wait for help; or when I experience pain, suffering or an illness, either my own or that of another.

Whatever the situation, these are times when I feel God is powerfully at work.

In living with and taking care of vulnerable sisters, I also experience the holy in the simple and ordinary. Heavy days are part and parcel of life.

However, it is often in the midst of such days, when you least expect it, that a sister would say something very humorous that really gives us a great laugh and a good lift. We recognise all the more that our exchanges are not one-sided but quite mutual. We might be caring for them, but they also nourish us by bringing out the best in us!

This can take the form of seemingly small but significant little courtesies and kindnesses: a note and a Kit-Kat placed in an open envelope at my door. Such heart-to-heart statements of warm love and gratitude are *seen and heard*. Every gift is saying something very revealing of the giver and says *everything*. It lets me know that these small gifts of goodness are beyond words or price. They confirm not only God's holy operation, but also that virtue is its own reward.

I believe this really captures the essence of *true holiness*. God is in our everyday, moving and acting in, with and through, our *real circumstances*. When God is our *centre and focus*, then we are given all that we need for all we are called to do and the guidance for the many decisions we face daily.

Sr Regina McHugh was born in Raharney, Mullingar, Co. Westmeath. After secondary school in Loreto Mullingar, she trained as a nurse in Jervis Street Hospital, Dublin and as a midwife in Scotland. Regina spent some time nursing with Concern in Bangladesh and as Public Health Nurse on the Aran Islands. She subsequently entered the Poor Clare Community in Ennis, Co. Clare, where she has lived happily for thirty-two years.

60

Fr Peter McVerry

I do not find God anywhere; God finds me. The question for me is: 'Where do I look for God?'

Imagine a person sitting on a riverbank on a beautiful day, enjoying the sun. There is a child playing on the riverbank beside him. Suddenly the child falls into the river. The person on the river bank jumps in and rescues the child. What will the parents of that child do? Of course, they will go the hospital to assure themselves that their child is alright. But after that, what will the parents do? They will want to find that person to thank him/her for saving their child's life.

To look for God, we have to look not up into the sky, nor in our churches or mosques or synagogues, but around us: to look at the poverty, the suffering, the loneliness of those around us. That is where I have to look for God. When I reach out to try and take some of that suffering off their shoulders, then God will come to find me, to thank me for what I have done for God's children. And when God finds me, I meet God. When I meet God, I am filled with a peace and joy which is unshakeable.

I meet God in the pain of those around me.

Fr Peter McVerry SJ has been working with vulnerable young people in Dublin for the last forty years. As a social activist Peter is a strong advocate for those who have no voice in society. He has written extensively on issues relating to young homeless people, such as accommodation, drugs, juvenile justice, the Gardaí, prisons and education, and spoken on these issues to groups around the country.

Image © Christy McNamara

Martina Meskell

In Him we live and move and have our being. (Acts 17:28)

I believe that 'In us He lives and moves and has His being'.

I find God in:

- My deepest innermost core
- My waking, sleeping, restlessness
- My conscience
- My shared love with my husband
- Family gathered at the table
- Celebrations
- The twinkle in the aged azure eyes of my dad as he perfectly plays old tunes on his melodeon and sings 'Some enchanted evening', lovingly reminiscing on his first encounter with my dearly departed mother
- Relationships and interactions with my friends, work colleagues and students
- Music ... especially liturgical music, as I profoundly experience a special connection to Jesus in that sacred place, as He caresses my heart and soul with His powerful yet gentle touch
- My harp playing
- Life's struggles and challenges such as illness, death and conflict
- The strength and fortitude bestowed by Him upon me, enabling me to cope with life's unwelcome surprises
- Nature, universe and everything

God is down in the swamps and marshes ... beautiful, beautiful, beautiful God was breathing His love by a cut-away bog.

— 'The One' by Patrick Kavanagh

Martina Meskell has been married to her husband Séan for the last twenty-seven years and has three adult children. She loves music and up to recently directed her local parish choir, but unfortunately she has had to take a break due to health issues. Martina's faith is strong, centred on the belief that church is community and God is in the people, not the building.

Image © Christy McNamara

John Murray

I recall during our time in Beijing we attended 'underground' Mass in the Canadian Embassy; the Chinese don't really acknowledge the existence of the Catholic Church, but are happy to turn a blind eye to the celebration of Mass by expats once it's done discreetly.

We were blessed with a wonderful young priest, an American called Fr Albert, whose six-minute sermons were always thought-provoking. He reckoned that in an average day, God visited us about a dozen times, presenting us on each occasion with an opportunity to act and behave in a Christian way; to help a troubled friend, to be polite and courteous to those we met, to think about the plight of the homeless man or woman we passed by and how we could best help them, and so on.

Fr Albert was asking us to be conscious of the presence of this 'practical' God. I'd like to be able to say that I have followed his advice to the letter but, alas, there are too many days when I don't meet the challenge and his criteria.

My faith, though, does help me to deal with the ups and downs of life in a measured way and I'm reminded all the time of my mother's advice that all things happen for a reason, and are related to the will of God.

John Murray is an Irish journalist and broadcaster. He co-presented *Morning Ireland* from 2006–2010. His radio show, *The John Murray Show* was enjoyed by many listeners from 2010–2015. He can currently be heard on Radio 1's *Weekend Sport* programme. He has two children, Stephen and Catherine.

Image © Giles Norman

Nuala Murray

I think that we see God through the lenses of our own lives: cultural, psychological or any other factors that have a hand in shaping our lives. Therefore finding God in the midst of life can be difficult. A lot of the spiritual traditions put the emphasis on seeking God, always seeking, and this has acted as a safeguard in my own life. So where do I seek God? At a general level I would have to say everywhere, because I truly believe that God's spirit, the Holy Spirit, imbues all created matter. The Rule of St Benedict suggests that we should treat the utensils of the kitchen as if they were as sacred as the vessels of the altar. I find this extraordinarily rich in what it suggests. We have all got lost in the midst of preparing a meal, baking, hoovering, even ironing; there is a solace in this kind of active solitude that brings me into the companionship of God and community of all householders before me.

Finally, I think we experience God in those moments when life leaves us speechless, when we are moved to tears of joy or tears of helplessness before tragedy and pain. I like to think that tears are literally the 'expression' of God in our lives; when life is too much and words are too little God takes the initiative and speaks. Tears flow one into the next, self-created images, boundaries and inhibitions melt and God speaks in God's own fashion: universally, timelessly and creatively. I would have to say therefore that I find God most powerfully present when I allow myself to break down before the highs and lows of life, and dare to believe that God is indeed truly with me.

Nuala Murray is married to Paddy and they have three children, Simon, Anna and Ronan. She lives in Quin, Co. Clare. She is an accredited spiritual director and school chaplain. She loves to spend time in Glenstal Abbey and is an Oblate of the Order of St Benedict.

Image © John Kelly

Pius Murray

Landscape is a living presence, with which I have a great affinity. I love the landscape! Walking in a silent landscape allows me to commune with nature and be in harmony with the universe. The cracked, cratered, lunar Burren is the landscape with which I am most familiar. Permit me to describe instead a visit to the Mahon Falls, in the Comeragh Mountains, Co. Waterford. It being my first visit, I was intent on walking attentively and taking it all in. As I stood at the entrance to the valley leading to the waterfall, I became aware of the rocky crags on both sides, which looked like silent sentinels on duty, vetting yet another visitor. I paused and asked their permission to enter, and when I felt welcome I proceeded on my journey. As I made my way towards the waterfall, along the rough track, I was met by the sounds of the rushing stream flowing in the opposite direction. At the base of Mahon Falls, I clambered upwards for a short distance over enormous boulders, and found a rocky waterside seat. While inhaling and exhaling the sweet, fresh, invigorating mountain air, I meditated. Presently I descended to the deep rock-pool into which the waterfall spilled and immersed myself completely in the cool water.

One could not but connect with the spirit – fiery and energetic – which is within each of us, in a landscape such as the Comeraghs, where God is close!

Pius Murray lives in Corofin, Co. Clare. He organises and leads inspirational walks in the Burren and Cliffs of Moher Geopark and on Inisheer, which enable walkers to reconnect with nature and with the spirituality of the landscape (www.coisceimanama.ie). He is a member of Pilgrim Paths Ireland (www.pilgrimpath.ie) and the Burren Ecotourism Network (www.burren.ie).

Image © Norman McCloskey

Maolíosa Ní Chléirigh

Tagaim ar Dhia nuair a nochtar gan coinne giorria, nó sionnach, earc sléibhe nó frog nó ainmhí fiáin rúnda eile dom. Teachtairí Dé iad, dar liom; an anáil céanna ag sní trínn.

Tagaim ar Dhia in áiteanna iargúlta. Feicim an tsíoraíocht greannta ar chloch, na finnéithe ársa sin a insíonn scéal na beatha.

Tagaim ar Dhia nuair a fheicim cornán caisil ag fás faoi chrann nó ar chlaí. Feicim foirfeacht na beatha agus gach uile ní ann.

Tagaim ar Dhia sna blátha agus sna luibheanna sa gháirdín a thagann ar ais go dílís bliain i ndiaidh bliana: Feicim dílseacht Dé iontu.

Feicim Dia sna blátha fiáine a fháisceann cothú as scoilt sa stroighin. Feicim diong-bháilteacht Dé iontu.

Tagaim ar Dhia i mbarróg grámhar, nuair a bhraithim cuisle eile ag bualadh: an anáil céanna ag sní trínn. Tagaim ar Dhia i ngníomhartha beaga fánacha grá. Feicim grá Dé iontu.

Tagaim ar Dhia i súile linbh. Feicim soineantacht Dé ag stánadh amach astu.

Braithim Dia i gcomhluadar, i gcaint, i gcómhrá, i gciúnas grámhar nuair a bhraithim an anáil céanna ag sní trínn go léir.

Maolíosa Ní Chléirigh was born in Galway. Her family moved to Dublin when she was six and she grew up there, in an Irish-speaking family. She has a degree in Irish and Spanish. She is a mother of two, a teacher and a writer of children's books. / Rugadh Maolíosa Ní Chléirigh i nGaillimh. Bhog a clann go Baile Átha Cliath nuair a bhí sí sé bliana d'aois agus tógadh ansin le Gaeilge í. Ta céim aici sa Ghaeilge agus sa Spáinnis. Is máthair, scríbhneoir agus múinteoir í. Tá beirt pháistí aici. Scríobhann sí leabhair do pháistí.

Image © Norman McCloskey

Nóirín Ní Riain

Everything that I see, hear, touch, feel, taste, speak, think, imagine, is completing a perfect circle which God has drawn.

— Meister Eckhart (1260–1328)

This prayer, from one of the world's greatest mystics, monks and scholars, has taught me so much about finding God through each and every one of our senses. Since God created us, most of us blessed with all five senses, surely that Divine Creator wants to have an intimate relationship with us through these generous pathways to the soul.

Our senses are marvellous guides that gently steer us into the inner world of the heart; each one of us will have a unique belonging to one or other of these sensual and sensuous thresholds.

For me, that sense-world is and always has been the ear; through the sense of hearing, I can frequently draw near to the message that the Spirit is trying to whisper into my ear.

The Spirit of God is aural and noisy, Jesus promised with great certainty. In one transformative, revealing description of the Spirit, the Christian hero tells us that although the source and destiny of the Spirit are elusive, what is sure, certain and beyond all doubt is that it can be heard:

The Spirit blows where it wills, you do not know where it comes from or where it goes, but you hear the SOUND of it (Jn 3:8).

Therefore, may we who seek and search for God take time to experience the sacredness of every sound that tickles our ears from this day onwards.

Nóirín Ní Riain, an internationally acclaimed spiritual singer, is also a theologian and author. The subject of her doctoral studies was a theology of listening, for which she coined the term 'Theosony', meaning the Sound of God. She lives at the Benedictine monastery of Glenstal Abbey, where she continues to offer workshops/retreat days on various themes.

Brendan O'Brien

The spirit of the Lord is on me, for he has anointed me to bring the good news to the afflicted. He has sent me to proclaim liberty to captives, sight to the blind, to let the oppressed go free, to proclaim a year of favour from the Lord. (Lk 4:18–19)

In the past few years I have been fortunate enough to bring some of my students to the township of Missionvale in the city of Port Elizabeth in the Eastern Cape in South Africa. In the township Sr Ethel Normoyle works tirelessly with the poorest of the poor. Frequently, these words from Luke and Isaiah resonate with me because of the compassion of Sr Ethel and her community care workers. I believe the preservation of the dignity of the human person is at the heart of Luke's words. In Missionvale the dignity of the human person comes first. Personally, I find God at the centre of it. We too are sent out. If ever you are seeking God you will find him in Missionvale, where many walk humbly with him.

In my daily life as a teacher of Religious Education, I find God in my encounters with the young people I teach. I find God in the joy with which they live out their lives, the cheerful way in which they greet each other, the support they unreservedly give to each other in times of illness, bereavement or disappointment, and when they try to grapple with the ever-present questions of meaning that are constantly discussed in the classroom.

If you stand on the beach in Fanore in North Clare and, on a fine day as the sun sets, look out to sea and breathe in the beauty of it all, you may find God in the stillness. I do.

Brendan O'Brien is from Ennis, Co. Clare. He co-presents the *Beyond Belief* programme on Clare FM. He has been a teacher since 1990 and is currently teaching in St Anne's Community College, Killaloe, Co. Clare. He was instrumental in delivering training for the Junior Certificate programme in Religious Education.

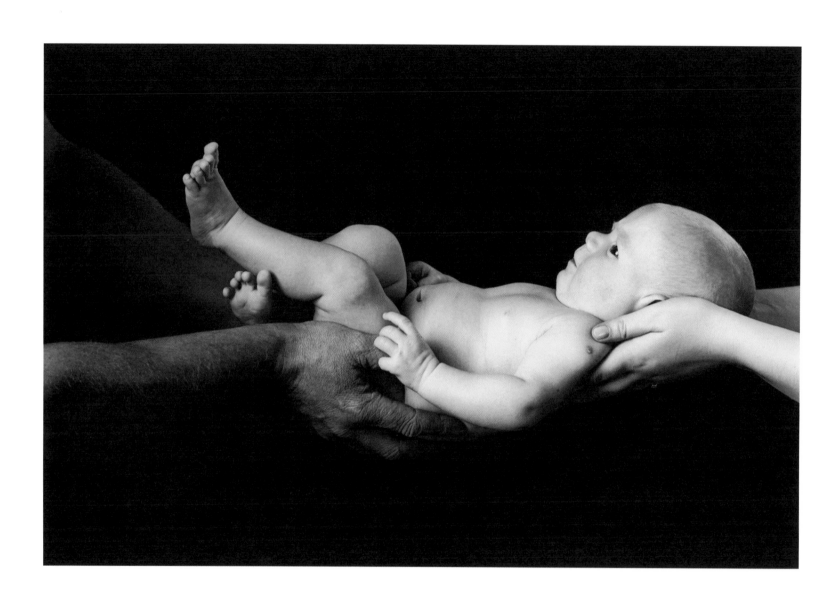

Rita O'Brien

One day a woman came into the hospital where I work for her routine ultrasound scan of her baby at thirty-six weeks' gestation. The baby's heartbeat had stopped. The doctor told her gently that her baby had died. I sat in silence with this lady. When she lifted her head we held each others' gaze for what seemed like an eternity. I felt God in that gaze.

When I worked in the Neonatal Intensive Care Unit, sometimes out of the blue I was touched by a wave of calm and I could feel God between my hands and the baby's tiny body.

On Sundays, tucked away in our little Godly playroom overhead, the congregation below, I sit on the floor in a circle with the children and in silence we 'get ready' to hear the story. Those precious moments recharge my batteries for the whole week.

I know deep down, even though I'm not always aware or tuned in, that every one of us and all of creation are connected by this great Mystery that we call God.

Rita O'Brien is married to a farmer and lives in the countryside. Her most important job is being a mother to two amazing boys, Tom and Conor. She has mostly worked as a midwife and neonatal nurse, but more recently changed career to bereavement counsellor in the Maternity Hospital.

Image © John Kelly

Daniel O'Connell

Last thing at night, before I go to bed, I call into the children's bedrooms. We have two boys: one is five and the other is seven. I love this final visit. They are always fast asleep, tucked up safe and sound. They are so peaceful and perfect at this time. In these visits, I feel such a sense of well-being and my heart swells. There is a profound sense of connection to them; my life bound up with theirs.

In these visits I forget about the day that has gone by and I don't think about the one to come; all I know is this moment. Here I am forgetful of myself. I feel free, simply enveloped in love for these two boys. And it is here, in these moments, that I find God.

I believe that God is love (1 Jn 4:8) and where there is love, there is God. My children help me notice and cherish the presence of love. In this way, I believe they are somewhat sacramental; their lives reveal the presence of God. Their very existence reorientates my whole life and invites me into love. They ask me to join them in the present moment, for example to wrestle with them on the floor and find delight in doing it. When we explore together the world of Power Rangers, they are asking me to let go of my busyness and take myself less seriously. They help me into a world in which I become less attached to myself and more open to them and their world of wonder and possibility. I believe their love helps me notice God – who is love – loving me, in and through my children.

Dan O'Connell is married and has two young children. He lives in Ennis and is a lecturer in Religious Education at Mary Immaculate College, Limerick. He has co-written the new *Grow in Love* programme for junior and senior infants in primary schools.

Image © John Kelly

80

Chris O'Donnell

'Where do I not find God?' would be an easier question to answer. I say this because, for me, God is a constant presence, found in almost everything and everyone. Of course there are situations, moments and certain people at a given time in which it is a real challenge to find God. Trusting in God's presence in these more difficult moments and people is an ongoing struggle.

It is easy for me to find God in my family, friends, pets and sports. On a daily basis I also find God in the following ways:

- In an expression of truth, a moment of genuine, loving honesty.
- In an example of beauty, a star-filled night or lovely sunset.
- In any act of goodness, compassion and solidarity.
- In a moment of genuine love and affection, something as simple as a child's hand held caringly.
- In moments when I am moved beyond myself by a piece of music, singing or a story.
- In the moment when out of nowhere I remember something important or helpful.
- In moments of silence, solitude and prayer.

And finally, as this project is in aid of Focus Ireland, I can say I found God when a homeless man shared with me his faith and this introductory passage from the Gideon Bible:

Read it to be wise, believe it to be safe, and practise it to be holy. It contains light to direct you, food to support you, and comfort to cheer you. It is the traveller's map, the pilgrim's staff, the pilot's compass, the soldier's sword and the Christian's charter.

Chris O'Donnell is from Adare in Co. Limerick. Outside of his family, friends and faith, his passions are sport, music, spirituality and young people. Along with his colleague Aoife Walsh he currently works in youth ministry in the Limerick diocese.

Tom O'Halloran

My favourite story comes from a friend of mine, Dermot, who once met a homeless man looking for help near Westminster Cathedral, in central London. The man fitted the stereotypical description of homeless people at that time. Dermot said to him: 'Aren't you from Kerry?' The conversation finished about an hour later, at which point the homeless man took a handful of half-crowns from his pockets and said: 'These are coins of the people who pass you by, who throw you a few coins but do not care about you.'

I often find God in those who have not known much love. A conversation on where God is to be found will seldom touch those who are the cast-offs of society, but a caring presence will. Ten years as an immigrant chaplain and six years on the missions have left me with no illusions about easy answers to the complexity of homelessness, but a willingness to reach out to people worse off than ourselves is essential for all who embrace a vision of all people living with dignity.

We are familiar with the loud cry of our culture: 'I'm not religious but I am spiritual.' This claim seems to ditch traditional religious practice. Yet finding spirituality without a religious tradition can be an agonising and restless search for many. Structures, for all their faults, offer a place to nurture spirituality. An awareness of God's presence may be elusive today, but if the major religions are understood according to their spiritual wisdom, this does not have to be true.

For me finding God involved catching up with my spirit. Did Jesus not say it all when he invited us to come to him and find rest in him? I seek to inhabit that space as much as I can.

I also find wholeness in my garden, inhaling its diversity and savouring its beauty. Finally I find God, mostly without knowing it at the time, in the love I receive from others, especially friends and family. At the end of each day, I like to reflect on the beauty, challenges and grace that the day has offered.

Tom O'Halloran was born in East Clare. Since ordination in 1975 Tom has worked in pastoral ministry in London, Zimbabwe, Chicago and now for thirteen years in Ireland as a parish priest in Borrisokane, Co. Tipperary. As spiritual guide of AISGA he seeks to discern where the hints of God are in his daily life. He has spent ten years working as a chaplain with immigrants and six as a volunteer missionary.

Image © Norman McCloskey

84

Daniel O'Leary

My tender Mother-God, another day begins with the light of your face in mine. You are the love that fills my senses as I awake to your desire. You are the hope in my eyes, the wonder in my heart, the blood in my veins, the tears that flow. With each new breath our hearts entwine. This dawning day reveals again your naked longing for your Word made flesh in me.

With a lover's tender fingers you untie the knots of my morning mind, you untwist the twisted tangles of love gone wrong, you press me to your healing heart and kiss away the hurting. We are intimate as water is in wine, as the holy bread is in our Sunday bodies, as lovers are in their innocent and everlasting moment.

Oh my Artist of beauty, you are my seed and blossom, the first snowdrop in my slow winter, the sure summer in my precarious and precious life. You reach for and delight in me; blindly you adore me. I do not need to find you. My deepest me is already and always you. With you I overflow into all creation as the chalice would with the sea.

Daniel O'Leary is a priest of the diocese of Leeds, UK and an author and teacher. He is a well-known conference speaker and retreat director. He is also the author of *The Happiness Habit* (2015) and *The Healing Habit* (2016), both Columba Press.

Donagh O'Meara

Paddy Kavanagh, the Monaghan poet, spoke about God being in the bits and pieces of life, 'a kiss here, a laugh there, and sometimes tears'. God for me is in the ordinary experiences of every day. I sometimes at night look back over the day and can trace moments when something greater was happening. God often arrives in an uplifting letter or card from somebody, saying thanks for a kindness done, or in a word of encouragement from an unexpected place.

I worked for a while in South Africa and it wasn't easy work. There was terrible poverty and every day was a challenge. I often found myself wondering: where is God in all of this? Why does God allow this to happen? One moment sticks out for me. A little boy of nine years of age used to call to my house regularly for food and one day, as it was school time, I asked him, 'Why aren't you at school?' He said, 'I have no shoes to go to school.' Luckily I was able to get shoes from Sr Ethel for him. He tried them on, and no words can convey the look in his eyes as he said 'I will be able to go to school now' and gave me a big hug. In the joy and love of that little boy God was present.

It is in the sacred encounters of every day that God is present.

Donagh O'Meara is a native of Clarecastle. He is a priest of the diocese of Killaloe and works in the parishes of Bodyke, Tuamgraney and Ogonnelloe.

Image © Giles Norman

Brent Pope

I was always aware of God and spirituality in my life. I know that sounds like a ridiculous thing to say, but religion played such an important part in my upbringing. With a surname like *Pope* I guess I had to be Catholic, huh? My father Mick was head of the local parish council for many years, and religion remains a huge part of who he is; even to this day Dad and Mum both have an amazing faith. For me it's not about one specific religion, despite being brought up a strict Catholic, and it's not about attending church every week either; to me it's about what I believe to be God's greatest message: 'That you always treat others as you would have them treat you.' I try to embrace that message every day.

I would like to think that God and God's children consider me a kind, empathetic person, that in my time on this world I am making a difference to someone else's life too. In that regard my charity work is a huge part of who I am as well; maybe in the end that is God's purpose for me. I still believe that my God is watching over me every day, guiding me. Nobody is perfect and we all slip up – after all, to err is human – but if we try and live our lives as kind, thoughtful, caring people, then in my mind at least that is what God wants from me, whatever religion, faith, or beliefs I have.

I also find God in nature and children, in the beauty and purity of a young child's laughter, in the buzzing of the bees and the colours of the seasons. God is nature, God is innocence. Today we live in a hustle-and-bustle world: everything is about change. People need to slow down and take stock of what is really important in this world, like the beautiful planet that God created, that some are intent on destroying, and the beautiful creatures and people that inhabit it. At least that is where I find 'my God'.

Brent Pope is a New Zealand-born rugby player, professional rugby coach, and one of Ireland's best known and most respected media personalities. Brent has been prominent as one of RTÉ's main rugby pundits since 1993. He is also a children's book author and a charity worker.

Image © Norman McCloskey

Tom Ryan

I sit here in the Adoration Chapel of Ennis Cathedral at three o'clock in the morning, as I do every Saturday morning. I sit here with one other person and with Jesus, present in the Blessed Sacrament. There is stillness at this hour; there is the darkness leading into light. There is time to think, to wonder and to pray. I hear God speaking to me in the stillness; in the sound of the birds, in the occasional car that passes by, in the odd outburst of revelry that comes from the young people making their way home from the nightclub. This is the hour of the week when I feel closest to God.

As I open the door to let in the next couple for the following hour of prayer Rosie remarks that it is a nice morning, and it is. I thank God for the opportunity to sit with him, and he with me, and just to be in each other's company and to be aware of each other. I look forward to three o'clock in the morning; it is the fastest hour of the week.

In the morning, let me know your love, O Lord.
(Psalm 142)

Be still and know that I am God.
(Psalm 46)

Tom Ryan, a native of Ennis, is a priest of the diocese of Killaloe. Ordained in 1984, he began ministry as a curate in St Eugene's Cathedral, Derry and at present is parish priest in Shannon, Co. Clare.

Image © Christy McNamara

Image © Norman McCloskey

Ronan Scully

I find God in helping others. I recall one cold morning when I worked with Mother Teresa's Missionaries of Charity in Calcutta, or Kolkota as it is known now. I was in Sealdah railway station and saw a middle-aged woman lying on the ground. She was suffering from leprosy. Her fingers were falling off, as was one of her feet, and she was trembling from the cold. She was trying to cover her body with a torn blanket so that no one would see her deformity, but couldn't. So many people passed by there, but no one helped. I whispered to myself, 'God, why are you giving so much pain to this beautiful woman? Why are you not helping her?'

Then I realised that God sent me to help this person. I ran to help her cover her body, then flagged down a taxi. The driver, seeing the predicament, sped through the streets of Calcutta to the Mother Teresa house, Kali-ghat, also known as the house of the dying. The woman's name was Mara Nivad-Davy. On that journey she told me her life's story, one of abject poverty and horror.

I carried her from the taxi into Kali-ghat and stood near her feet as the Mother Teresa sisters cleaned her and cared for her. Half of her left foot had been completely eaten away by maggots. The bones were sticking out of her foot, and some of these had even been worn away because Mara had used her foot to drag herself along. The foot was amputated that day, and Mara died a few days later, surrounded by love and prayers.

That event changed me a lot. God gave me the dream to help those in need in our community and in our world. That day I realised that a dream is one thing, but trying to achieve it is another thing altogether. I am still doing my best, but I need help and I need your help and at the end of the day we all need one another's help. I find God all the time, especially when helping others in need. If you see anybody who requires help, don't just pass by; try to help, if possible. Maybe God sent you to help them. Maybe that's where you find God!

Ronan Scully is originally from Clara in Co. Offaly. He is married to Jacqui O'Grady and they have two daughters, Mia and Sophie, adopted from Ethiopia. He is Irish humanitarian charity Gorta–Self Help Africa's Regional Representative for the midlands and west of Ireland. He has authored two books, *Hold That Thought* (2010) and *Time Out* (2013). He also writes an inspirational weekly column called 'Thought for the Week' for *The Galway Independent*.

Seán Sexton

When faced with this question the first thing that comes to mind is the vastness and immensity of the night sky. It brings to my mind, straight away, the words of Psalm 8: 'When I look at your heavens, the work of your fingers, the moon and the stars which you have established; what are human beings that you are mindful of them, mortals that you care for them?' Occasionally I make a point of observing the International Space Station orbiting the earth at about ninety-minute intervals. I am fascinated by how clearly visible it is even though it is more than 200 miles away, but perhaps I ought not be surprised, given that it's the size of a football pitch.

As human beings we are made in the image and likeness of God. Little wonder that every day gives me opportunities to see God's reflection in the people I meet. I have a friend who spends his days in a wheelchair. I find God in the warmth of his welcome and in his gentle presence, which blow away my own petty concerns. I find God, too, in the generous parents who, with unlimited love, enrich the lives of their special needs children. And I have no words to describe the anguish of those bereaved by suicide, which brings me face to face with the God of Calvary.

Sometimes I find God in the direct, sharp language of a poet. Raymond Carver is an American poet who lived a topsy-turvy life. In his early days he struggled with alcoholism and later with cancer. The following lines, from 'In Switzerland', suggest to me that he was on God's wavelength:

All of us, all of us, all of us
trying to save
our immortal souls, some ways
seemingly more round-
about and mysterious
than others.

Seán Sexton grew up in Lissycasey, Co. Clare, attended St Flannan's College, Ennis and was ordained as a priest in 1965. Early in his priesthood he travelled to Swansea to pursue postgraduate studies in Youth Leadership and Organisation. He returned to Ennis and worked as a chaplain in the Vocational School for five years. He was one of the founding members of Clare Youth Service, where he worked as Director and Board Member from 1974 to 2008. He is currently parish priest of Inagh, Kilnamona, Co. Clare.

Image © John Kelly

Fr Willie Teehan

At 2.30 a.m. on Saturday, 14 February 2015, my brother Con rang me to say that our nephew Brian was missing in Galway after a night out with college friends. The following days, with family, neighbours, friends, classmates and teammates, were spent searching the city for him and we found his body early on Sunday morning.

It was a most painful experience that shattered our lives, and we still struggle to come to terms with the loss of 'a gentle giant' who was a treasured member of our family. He pursued a career in journalism because of his sense of justice and wanting to be a voice for the poor.

His funeral took place on Ash Wednesday and throughout the forty days of Lent I too asked the question of God that Jesus asked on Good Friday: 'My God, why have you abandoned me?'

That powerful question, asked by so many people in similar tragic situations, reminds me that I'm not alone on the journey, that there is a bigger picture and that light ultimately overcomes darkness. I have glimpsed the love of God in the Easter scriptures and in the support of colleagues, family and friends at this very challenging time. One friend was most helpful when she said, 'It's a mystery to be lived with, not a problem to be solved.'

As I look out from my home here in Templederry to the hills of Hantsgrove, Chalkhill and Garryglass, I often reflect on the following prayer, which I find inspirational.

Lift us up, strong Son of God, that we may see further. Strengthen our faith that we may see beyond the horizon.

— Bede Jarrett OP

Willie Teehan is from Dunkerrin, Co. Offaly, where he attended the local national school and went then to the C.B.S., Roscrea. He studied for the priesthood in St Patrick's College, Carlow and was ordained for the Killaloe diocese in June 1984. He feels privileged to serve as parish priest of Templederry in Co. Tipperary.

Elma Walsh

To me, God is like a friend. I can talk to Him and tell Him my worries, thank Him when things go right, but equally I give out to Him when I see injustices.

I was cross and angry with Him each time Donal was diagnosed with cancer; I gave out to Him and ranted when Donal was diagnosed terminal; but after a while I could see the graces He gave Donal in being able to cope so well with his short life on earth.

While Donal really wanted to live and travel the world, he did accept what was handed to him in this life. He always said that 'God has me by the hand and when I die I will be in His arms.' For that I was grateful to God; also that Donal was given the opportunity to tell others, young people especially, to appreciate their lives and live them to the full.

I suppose I find God in the good and the bad of everyday life, there to encourage and help us in the decisions we make. Ultimately we will make the decision, but in doing so, we also know which one is the right one or the wrong one.

Like a real friend He will guide us to a point, but in the end it is up to each of us how we take that guidance.

In May 2013, Donal Walsh lost his cancer battle at sixteen years of age. Prior to his passing he appeared as a guest on Brendan O'Connor's *Saturday Night Show* and won the hearts of a nation as he pleaded with the youth of Ireland not to take their own lives through suicide. His parents, Elma and Fionnbar, set up the Donal Walsh #Livelife Foundation in order to continue his anti-suicide message.

Image © John Kelly

Fionnbar Walsh

Growing up I was taught that God is everywhere! To a child this is easy to accept but difficult to understand. Even to an adult there can be difficulty in understanding this.

Having travelled through a four-year journey with our son Donal, as he battled cancer and lived life honestly up to his death, there were times I asked and bartered with God to deliver us from the cross we were bearing. You don't barter with God; you learn, from the other child patients, that the line from the cross, 'Not my will but yours be done' is real.

Donal died with great dignity, leaving a legacy that has inspired many, but mainly the youth of this nation. They are asking us to visit and talk to them, to 'continue the conversation that Donal started' with that now-famous interview with Brendan O'Connor. What was that interview about? The gift that is life! We have it and it is a gift and we should value it. Donal had no choice in the sentence he was given, but he chose to live his final months, weeks and days right up to the end. He was up with his friends watching a movie until nine at night on Friday, and then he died at eight p.m. on Sunday night.

The gift he has left us is finding God through those that he has left an imprint on. It could be a seventy-year-old or a transition year student. These people tell us their stories and then I realise the legacy of Donal is part of God's story. Donal's journey, climbing God's mountains, continues to be where I find God.

In May 2013, Donal Walsh lost his cancer battle at sixteen years of age. Prior to his passing he appeared as a guest on Brendan O'Connor's *Saturday Night Show* and won the hearts of a nation as he pleaded with the youth of Ireland not to take their own lives through suicide. His parents, Elma and Fionnbar, set up the Donal Walsh #Livelife Foundation in order to continue his anti-suicide message.

Image © John Kelly

Willie Walsh

I have been asked where do I find God in my daily life. Obviously it is a difficult question because I can never find God in the same way as I find other things in life, through the senses. So when I speak of finding God I think I mean what helps, what gives meaning to my belief in God. In that sense I find God in people, especially in the sheer goodness, generosity and kindness of people. I find God especially in the people whom I love and who love me.

In a strange way I also find God in the people whom I struggle to love, in the poor, in people who have been broken and abused by life. I say in a strange way because while I often wonder how a God whom we claim to be loving can allow this pain and suffering, yet at the same time if there were no God then life, and indeed my own life, would be meaningless, and I don't think I could cope with that.

Sometimes I struggle to find God in the midst of all this pain and suffering across the world. Yet belief in God keeps me going. It is not a blind belief which quells all doubts. It is rather a decision of mind and heart that belief in a God who treasures each one of us makes sense of, and gives meaning and purpose to, my life.

Willie Walsh was Bishop of Killaloe from 1994–2010. He is admired by many for his willingness to speak openly and honestly about many controversial issues within the Catholic Church. Bishop Walsh has recently written a memoir, entitled *No Crusader* (Columba Press).

Image © Norman McCloskey

Image © Christy McNamara

Image © Norman McCloskey

Photographers

Christy McNamara

Christy McNamara is a photographer, musician and artist, a teller of stories. He currently divides his time between his home in Spancilhill, County Clare and New York City.

His work has been widely exhibited both at home and abroad and can be found in both public and private collections. The images selected here are drawn from a larger body of work made over the last twenty-five years. He remains faithful to shooting in the classic way on older film format cameras.

He has been commissioned by many leading publications, recording artists and corporate clients, including Aer Lingus, Guinness, Coca-Cola, the Department of Education, U2 and The Pogues.

www.christymcnamara.com

Norman McCloskey

Norman McCloskey has been photographing the landscape of Kerry and West Cork for over twenty-five years. Having graduated in Photography from IADT in 1995, he went on to work in the commercial and editorial area of the photography business for eighteen years before opening his own busy gallery in Kenmare. The gallery showcases the latest landscape work from Kerry, West Cork and beyond, alongside his own publication *Parklight* which was published in 2013.

www.kerrylight.com

Image © John Kelly

Image © Giles Norman

106

John Kelly

Working out of the west of Ireland, John Kelly is an evocative and original multi award-winning photographer. As staff photographer with *The Clare Champion*, he has chronicled the life of Clare over the past two and a half decades. His unique photographs scratch beneath the surface of everyday activity within the county.

Kelly's photographs have appeared in many publications and his work backboned the acclaimed publication, *The Scattering*. For that project, Kelly travelled to England, Belgium, Australia, New Zealand and Papua New Guinea to record the story of those who left Clare for further fields.

www.johnkellyphotography.ie

Giles Norman

Giles Norman is known for his black and white landscape photography of Ireland. His distinctive black and white collection captures the beauty and intrigue of Irish life and landscape. His impressive body of work represents over twenty-nine years of capturing images across Ireland, including Dublin and the Wild Atlantic Way. His work has been displayed in embassies, celebrities' homes, hotels and financial centres across the world.

Giles Norman was raised in Ireland and lives with his family in Kinsale, Co. Cork. He is a self-taught artist. He started taking photos in his early teens and even created his own darkroom in his attic. He set up a small gallery in idyllic Kinsale, where he met his wife Catherine, the business brains behind this inspiring artist.

Instead of a brush, Giles takes his 35mm Nikon to paint images of the Irish landscape that evoke a purity of vision, mostly stripped of man-made intrusion. His photos open a window into Ireland's dramatic scenery. Preferring to keep his pictures 'real', he shuns the special effects of modern photography.

www.gilesnorman.com

Image © Giles Norman

Where do you find God?